THE FORWARD LIFE

*Moving Beyond Your Past
Into God's Promises*

BERNARD TRIPPETT

The Forward Life: *Moving Beyond Your Past Into God's Promises*
Copyright 2014 by Bernard Trippett

Publisher's Cataloging-in-Publication Data

Trippett, Bernard, 1976-

ISBN: 978-1500813611

Scriptures used are from the King James Version of the Bible.

Published in the United States of America.

TABLE OF CONTENTS

Introduction   1

Chapter 1: One Thing   3

Chapter 2: Move Forward   6

Chapter 3: Stuck   12

Chapter 4: Your Red Sea   16

Chapter 5: What Are You Doing Here?   20

Chapter 6: First Step   25

Chapter 7: Forgiveness—A Forward Act   28

Chapter 8: Forward From Excuses   32

Chapter 9: Loss: The Revolving Door   34

Chapter 10: Your Setback, His Setup   37

Chapter 11: His Truth—The Perspective   40
Helper

Chapter 12: Living it Daily   42

Chapter 13: Ruling Over Your Thoughts   48

Chapter 14: The Double   51

Chapter 15: Time to Finish, Time to Live   53

Salvation   55

About the Author   61

Purpose   63

This book is dedicated to my wife, Kesha L. Trippett, who is lovely and full of grace. I never realized the depth of strength God has given to her until now. I never realized fully why her nickname is "Soldier" until now. She is the epitome of a forward life. I love you dearly, yet God loves us more.

INTRODUCTION

Who could God use any better than the Apostle Paul to supply this profound revelation? "As for Saul, he made havoc of the church, entering into every house, and haling men and women committed them to prison" (Acts 8:3). Paul, who was formerly named Saul, an educated Pharisee, out of his own ignorance, heavily persecuted the church. He also consented, or took pleasure in, the stoning of Stephen, a young man full of faith and power, which God used to do many miracles. Even after he had an encounter with the Lord Jesus Christ and was blinded, one believer questioned Jesus' command to help him. Acts 9:13 says, "Then Ananias answered, Lord, I have heard by many of this man, how much evil he hath done to thy saints at Jerusalem". One can only imagine how this felt: The negative opinions of Christians and Pharisees, the consent to killing Stephen, all the persecution, and all the regret and pain of his past. Yet, in spite of all of his mistakes, God revealed to the Apostle Paul how to do…

CHAPTER 1:

One Thing

"Brethren, I count not myself to have apprehended: but this one thing I do, forgetting those things which are behind, and reaching forth unto those things which are before, I press toward the mark for the prize of the high calling of God in Christ Jesus" (Philippians 3:13-14). There is nothing greater than obtaining the prize of the high calling of God in Christ Jesus, which is what you and I were created to do. In spite of all he had done in life, the Apostle Paul had a life-changing revelation. He arrived at something so powerful and revolutionary, that above all, it became the one thing he did to achieve this high goal and reason for living. One thing.

Several changes occur when a woman is given in marriage, one of which is she receives a new name. She may have been a Ms. Smith, but she becomes a Mrs. Jones. She is no longer known by her past name, because she has a new one, establishing her as being part of a whole, new family, embarking upon an entirely new chapter of life. In Christ, you have a new life, in a new kingdom, governed by new laws and ruled by a good God and Father. You may have had setbacks. You may feel there's too much ground to cover at your age. You may have devastating experiences and losses in your past. Yet, there is still one thing you must do. You cannot change where you have been, but because you now serve a good and gracious God, His destination for your life is still ahead. God's promises are always in front of you, not behind you.

I have been in traffic many times and I have made mistakes while driving and other cars that surround me have as well. As a whole, we don't angrily pull over on the side of the road when we're cut off by another driver. Nor do we lose confidence in our driving abilities. The reality of those fleeting moments is, we have somewhere to go and those things are minor in comparison to our destination to work, to a ball game or any other plans we have. Traffic is similar to life. You have somewhere to go in life and all of the trials we experience are minor, in comparison to the destination of God's calling. You can decide to be consumed with the cut-offs of life, even your own, or you can do one thing.

CHAPTER 2:

Move Forward

In life, if you are going to accomplish anything, if you are going to finish anything, if you are going to receive any of God's promises, you must do one thing: you must move forward. How do I move forward? Moving forward is just what it is. It is not an emotion or mental state. In God, we move forward through a literal, God-directed action.

Forward is Action

The only thing that separates us from our past and a promise from God is an action. "But wilt thou know, O vain man, that faith without works is dead? Ye see then how that by works a man is justified, and not by faith only" (James 2:20, 24). Without your actions, your faith stands dead and unfruitful. When you apply the brakes to your vehicle, the car will stop. No matter the speed, the car will cease to move. It will obey you. If a room is dark and we want to see, we turn on the light and the darkness flees. The light will invoke its' power upon the darkness. When we put into action God's Word in our lives, the discouragement and bitterness will obey Him; they must let you go. When we say what He says, peace will come and the turmoil will stop. Go forward with your God-given gifts and God will back you. Praise God and watch His joy arise in your heart. When you act, God removes the obstacle, and in turn, you receive the blessing.

The challenge is believing the action will produce our expectation. Remember, this is not merely an action. This is an action directed by God. It is the action inspired by God to combat all of the evil, oppression and past pains that seek to overtake you.

One of the most notable quotes I've heard was in a movie called, *World War Z*, starring Brad Pitt. It is a movie about a highly infectious disease that was turning human beings into zombies, and Brad Pitt's quest to find the cure. Towards the beginning of the breakout, the zombies were in pursuit of Pitt and his family. They continued to run from the zombies and entered into a Manhattan apartment building. A generous family lets them into their home to hide, and for a moment, they were safe. However, minutes later, he tells the head of the family, "I think you should leave with us." The man is stunned at the notion, wondering why they can't stay where they are. Pitt responds, "Movement is life".

The man decides to stay where it was momentarily more comfortable, and everyone except his son was infected. He lost his life because he didn't move. You can miss God's promises if you don't move.

Thinking alone is not enough to change where you are. You must literally move. God's directive will always be an action. "Be not overcome of evil, but overcome evil with good" (Romans 12:21). This is not merely a saying or a simple gesture, but rather this is the resolution of God to be heeded and applied. Make the forward action with your purpose and sharing the Gospel. Make the forward action with using your gifts for the glory of God. Make the forward action within your vocation and in your relationships to make them better.

Forward actions go beyond our feelings, as does faith goes beyond what we see. God instructs us to walk by faith and not by sight. We don't wait until we see it, then, believe it. On the contrary, we believe it, and then we see it. You can't wait to feel something and then act. We must rather take action, then, the action will prove itself to be the remedy of God. The freedom, the power, joy, and peace of God will flood you. No action led by God is without these, giving us the end we so desired. God's desire for you to have a full, abundant life, all the days of your life, is even greater than your very own. Trust Him.

He shows no partiality, proving it by giving His best, His only begotten Son, for us all. What He directs you to do is not for you only, but to show His unfailing love toward others— through you. The result is a blessed people, and in the end, He is glorified. "Let your light so shine before men, that they may see your good works, and glorify your Father which is in heaven" (Matthew 5:16).

CHAPTER 3:

Stuck

Some of the tough experiences we face in life are a result of not moving forward. We stand still, paralyzed by our past, when although it is gone, we continue to allow it to presently live. It secretly controls our attitude, our daily decisions, our peace, and emotions. We won't let it go, so we let ourselves go instead. We cry, overeat and gain weight as a result of being rejected by someone. We don't let go of failures, so we continue to fail. We don't let go of the bad relationship, so we miss a good one. With all sensitivity, we could have loss a child, yet we allow fear to grip us into a belief and mindset not to try again. We did something wrong, yet we beat ourselves on the inside and continually pay dearly for the same crime.

Let it go—because God has.

Romans 8:28 says, "And we know that all things work together for good to them that love God, to them who are the called according to his purpose." Nothing that occurs in our lives is by coincidence. If God allowed it, there is something to learn from it, and His ultimate plan is that you richly benefit from it.

Actions of offense done in our past are stuck there. That "What they did to me" moment can't move, just as lifeless rocks that sit on the side of our driveway. We can spend our lives standing there, walking around them, or we can take our spouse's hand, and go inside to enjoy some popcorn and a good movie. Sin's power is in holding on to what God has already let go of. It is holding on to the past and what has been lost, when God has already established a redemptive plan to restore it. It is carrying the burden of not being good enough, when Jesus is enough alone.

God allowed me to meet a gentleman to see what stuck really was. He was raised in church and his Mom was devout Christian, a praying woman. When he was 21 years old, a preacher accused him of lying and stealing. He said the accusation offended him so, to the point it felt like a knife went deep on the inside of his chest and cut him straight across it. It appeared the knife was as a traumatic experience of offense, still there, not pulled away. It was stuck there, just as he allowed it. He had not yet allowed God to remove the knife of offense and divinely heal the wound. He didn't want anything to do with God or His people. The best of relationships, blessings, opportunities, and the life of God, daily passed him by. Time was moving without him. He merely existed, rehearsing the unchangeable, instead of abundantly living.

Stuck.

Some leave it up to time and say time will heal it, yet it will never heal quite right without a God-directed action. You still aren't the same and you cannot truly move forward without it. In his case, God could very well tell him to go speak to the preacher about the offense and that forward action then leads to a dialogue in which God moves and heals. "He healeth the broken in heart, and bindeth up their wounds" (Psalm 147:3). It requires the depth of healing that only comes from God, Who is the total Healer. Otherwise, as some athletes never bounce back to their normal, optimum play from certain injuries, you will never be the same, bearing fruit for God until you decide to truly move forward.

CHAPTER 4:

Your Red Sea

Don't stay in the place of what I call the *"In Between"*. This is the place of indecision. It is the place where we wrestle between two opinions. We are in between God's promises and what we must leave behind, even our inadequacies. Israel had the same dilemma, as they made their exodus from Egyptian slavery into the promise land (Exodus 14:9-12). While escaping, they arrived at the Red Sea and it appeared they couldn't go any farther. Their enemy was behind them and the Red Sea in front of them. They also knew they couldn't stay where they were or they would be killed. They faced a life-changing moment of decision at the Red Sea.

We all will have our own Red Sea. Your decision will ultimately define you and your life.

You will either live in the past, or live in God's promises. It will be the difference between you seeing your promise land, and actually entering into it. You will either be good, or become great. Your dreams will either become a reality, or they will remain inside of you.

The thoughts of wondering how will God help me, how will they respond, am I good enough, how will I get the resources, will it work, I have no clue what I am doing, and I'm not in control, will surely come. The people of Israel struggled at this very point, even telling Moses, "Is not this the word that we did tell thee in Egypt, saying, Let us alone, that we may serve the Egyptians? For it had been better for us to serve the Egyptians, than that we should die in the wilderness" (Exodus 14:12). You can imagine the emotions and fears the children of Israel and Moses were faced with. I am certain it was chaos, which we all have experienced in life. In the face of it all, God's response to us is as it was to Moses, with an action: "And the LORD said unto Moses, Wherefore criest thou unto me? Speak unto the children of Israel, that they go forward" (Exodus 14:15).

At this moment, God instructs Moses to use the rod in his hand He had already given him to split the Red Sea. In essence, God was telling Moses the way is already made. God's way is not made by man's hands, but His own, which we may not understand or see every time. Yet, God says go forward and see what I have done. The great Red Sea will split before you, and what appears impossible for you to overcome, isn't impossible for Me. In our times of decision, there are many ways of fear, but only one way of faith. Watch the turmoil and bondage from your past cease, and every obstacle move that is in front of you. As your action shows you believe Him, your faith provides the door for God to move and deliver. What has He revealed to you to do with what is in your hands? He wants to move your Red Sea, so that you can enter into His perfect will for your life.

CHAPTER 5:

What Are You Doing Here?

Then He said, "Go out, and stand on the mountain before the Lord. And behold, the Lord passed by, and a great and strong wind tore into the mountains and broke the rocks in pieces before the Lord, but the Lord was not in the wind; and after the wind an earthquake, but the Lord was not in the earthquake; and after the earthquake a fire, but the Lord was not in the fire; and after the fire a still small voice. So it was, when Elijah heard it, that he wrapped his face in his mantle and went out and stood in the entrance of the cave. Suddenly a voice came to him, and said, What are you doing here, Elijah?"(1 Kings 19:11-13). God asked the Prophet Elijah this question 40 days after he fled from Jezebel, who was plotting to take his life. This was the same Elijah God used to raise a young boy from the dead. This was the same Elijah that just called down fire from heaven as proof of who serves the true and living God. He was afraid. Anytime we are knowingly somewhere other than in the perfect will of God, we are paralyzed with fear. Even in his paralysis, God in His abundant mercy permitted him to remain there for a time. He even provided food during his time of questioning himself, fear and doubt.

For some of us, this is a mirror of our life. The losses have been deeply sorrowful, to the point we wonder why go forward because we feel only more pain awaits. You dare not move, but rather remain fearfully comfortable and complacent; opting to settle for what appears to require nothing of you. In the midst of our entire struggle, we hear the still, small voice of God, "What are you doing here?" At this point, remaining where you are in life will become detrimental to you and your calling. You can't stay where you are, and eventually, the provision where you are will dry up (1 Kings 17:6-7). God's desire is to move from what He has permitted, into what is perfect—His perfect will for you. Do not remain comfortable and afraid in His permissive will, but rather be courageous and have a hunger for His perfect will. The one that backs that small voice is more powerful than the setbacks and fears. He is more merciful and restoring than we can figure out. You can't stay there. It is time to overcome.

No Condemnation

One of the feelings that we can experience in this place is condemnation. Our sin or fear takes us there; condemnation convinces us to stay. God used us to do great and mighty things, yet we are shattered and ashamed that we, out of all people, missed the mark. Then, as a cracked glass can't hold water, we disqualify ourselves as being unfit to be used and unworthy of any blessing.

"*There is* therefore now no condemnation to them which are in Christ Jesus, who walk not after the flesh, but after the Spirit. Who shall lay anything to the charge of God's elect? *It is* God that justifieth." (Romans 8:1, 33). Water can't be held in a cracked glass, but it can within a perfect and complete one. God takes us out of sin, and by faith, puts us in Christ and we are justified. Jesus is the perfect glass, and in him, there is no condemnation. Through His finished work of cleansing us from our sin, we will always be counted worthy to the Father. We will always be counted qualified and righteous. No matter what you have done, you are still called in Christ to be poured and used to quench those that are thirsty.

"For the gifts and calling of God *are* without repentance" (Romans 11:29). The one that called you will never disqualify you.

CHAPTER 6:

First Step

"And the Lord said, If ye had faith as a grain of mustard seed, ye might say unto this sycamine tree, Be thou plucked up by the root, and be thou planted in the sea; and it should obey you" (Luke 17:6). The hardest action for us is the first step. It can feel like it is the hardest faith, however, once received, you can do the impossible. It is a step of faith to believe the Gospel and receive Jesus Christ. Yet after that action, a flood of God and His love comes into our hearts and changes us. You step out of who you were, into a new person in Christ. 2 Corinthians_5:17 says, "Therefore if any man *be* in Christ, *he is* a new creature: old things are passed away; behold, all things are become new." You step out of your sin and into His righteousness. You feel wealthy without money. You have peace and joy when it appears there's no reason to have it all. Salvation and all that comes with it is yours, including the love of God, power, joy, deliverance, wholeness, oneness with God again, prosperity, access, justification, right-standing with God, freedom, forgiveness, peace and authority. Words just cannot explain, yet you are not the same. It all came from one pivotal decision.

This is our model for entering into God's promises and for day-to-day living. It takes a step of faith to decide to live holy. It takes a step of faith to forgive a trusted friend or mentor, to love again after a depleting divorce, to start a business or ministry, even if you've failed before, or to continue applying for a job when the odds are against you. "Ah Lord GOD! behold, thou hast made the heaven and the earth by thy great power and stretched out arm, *and* there is nothing too hard for thee" (Jeremiah 32:17). If God said go forward, you can go forward.

His direction affirms He is with you and there is nothing too hard for Him. He will bless you. Once you make the first step to believe and yield to Him, He will step in with His ability to help you. You will move from fear into faith. You will step out of bondage into freedom. You will step out of selfishness, into His love. You will step out of your weakness and into His strength. Your step is your mustard seed faith, after which nothing is impossible, and every promise from God is obtained.

CHAPTER 7:

Forgiveness—A Forward Act

Forgiveness is one of God's most powerful tools we move forward with because its' sole intent is to set our relationships right again. Jesus Christ mediated us back to the Father through his death for our sins. We have been redeemed and God follows us with goodness and mercy (Psalm 23:6), always setting our relationship right with Him again and again. With the same mercy and goodness, God commands us to freely extend to others. "And if he trespass against thee seven times in a day, and seven times in a day turn again to thee, saying, I repent; thou shalt forgive him" (Luke 17:4). No matter the amount, God commands us to forgive again and again, even toward our toughest critic—ourselves. We must forgive ourselves and others of what God has already forgiven us both of. When we forgive to this extent like God, total forgiveness, people truly experience Him—The God Who truly will remember their sins no more.

"For as the heavens are high above the earth, So great is His mercy toward those who fear Him; As far as the east is from the west, So far has He removed our transgressions from us" (Psalm 103:12). This is God's perspective on forgiveness. He removes our sins as far as the east is from the west. They are far from us and we aren't known by them. He separates us from not only the crime of sin, but the due punishment that comes along with it.

"If" Grudges

"Let all bitterness, and wrath, and anger, and clamour, and evil speaking, be put away from you, with all malice: And be ye kind one to another, tenderhearted, forgiving one another, even as God for Christ's sake hath forgiven you" (Ephesians 4:31-32). "If" Grudges are a deadly source of bitterness and can ruin us: "If they would not have done this, I would be here by now." "If they wouldn't have let me go, I would be a lot farther." "Only if they would have stayed, I wouldn't be so bitter and depressed." "If I would have made a better decision, I wouldn't be where I am."

We now have a hard time moving on because the grudge has taken over our lives and our peace is dependent upon a person, not God. "And it shall come to pass, if thou shalt hearken diligently unto the voice of the LORD thy God, to observe and to do all his commandments which I command thee this day, that the LORD thy God will set thee on high above all nations of the earth: And all these blessings shall come on thee, and overtake thee, if thou shalt hearken unto the voice of the LORD thy God" (Deuteronomy 28:1-2). He alone gives the conditions that decide whether we have a victorious life and finish God's course for our lives. If we follow Him, He will exalt and bless us.

CHAPTER 8:

Forward From Excuses

Not moving forward communicates the belief that we are completely stuck, when we are not. God empowers us, not only with the wisdom of what to do, but also, by His Spirit, the strength required for the action. No matter what it is, The Holy Spirit, The Comforter, is here to provide unfailing help.

Sometimes we have "stuck excuses", yet it is a hard truth to admit that we're stuck because we want to be. We don't want to move. We say we can't let go, therefore, we excuse our poor decisions, disobedience, comfort, and mediocrity. We now don't have to face our fears because we've embraced them. We don't have to fight the good fight of faith because we're not in the ring, competing for the perfect will of God. Facing this truth should be humbling, yet not condemning. It should be constructive, not destructive. God reveals the truth to make us free, not to bind us.

Only ignorance is a legitimate excuse to a certain point—to the point we are revealed the way out. It is at that point God uncovers the source of our pain, fears, and at the same time, the action to solve it. It is now a question of making a God-inspired forward action. "But He gives more grace. Therefore He says: God resists the proud, but gives grace to the humble" (James 4:6). Humble yourself and submit to God. You must allow the rescuing power of God's grace to empower you onward into what He has called you to do.

CHAPTER 9:

Loss: The Revolving Door

Your life can be a revolving door because of loss. You can be fifty years old and still entertain a revolving door of a single moment that occurred twenty years ago. "Everything was headed in the right direction until it happened", we say, as it revolves in our minds. Your spouse left, your business closed, your dream house foreclosed, you were laid off from a leading company you were hopeful to retire from, or your faith isn't as strong as it use to be. These can all be revolving doors, revisiting them time and time again, whether on purpose, or through the devil seeking to oppress you. Revolving doors can cause depression, health issues and mental illnesses.

"Discretion will preserve you; understanding will keep you" (Proverbs

2:11); "He who gets wisdom loves his own soul; He who keeps understanding will find good" (Proverbs 19:8). Understanding is God's remedy for loss. If you keep it, it will keep you. It doesn't matter when we want to be restored, as much as it matters when God wants us to receive it. God is sovereign, all-powerful, all-knowing, all-wise and already has it prepared. He can and will make up for any loss you've experienced, for He has great gain ahead. As you seek Him, He will give you the actions to take that will take you on His path of restoration. "And I will restore to you the years that the locust hath eaten, the cankerworm, and the caterpillar, and the palmerworm, my great army which I sent among you" (Joel 2:25). He will tell you where to go, who to approach, the strategy and more, on your journey to restoration. As you act, understand that a good God always has a good plan to restore.

This will not only keep you, but keep you moving forward.

CHAPTER 10:

Your Setback, His Set Up

"And we know that all things work together for good to those who love God, to those who are the called according to His purpose" (Romans 8:28). Some things happen in life that we just can't explain. Yet, every setback will prove to be His set up. If you love God, It will have its' place in His plan.

I did not begin my collegiate career being admitted into standard courses. I started college in remedial English and Reading due to my low SAT scores in these areas. I felt I was losing credit time, having to take classes to learn how to read and write, which I thought I already knew. In remedial English, I would have to learn correct grammar and write short essays daily to clearly communicate a point on paper. I then moved on and was accepted into the standard English course. Out of all I could have had, my first professor was the head of the entire English Department. The very first class, my English professor asked the class to write an essay about ourselves. I scored an A-. From the first day, I was blessed. I had been writing essays daily, and now, a remedial class that appeared to be a hindrance and delay, turned out to help me succeed.

I was set up.

I went on to be recommended by the department head into Honors English, became a professional copywriter and God now uses this gift of writing to change lives, sharing the Good News of Jesus Christ.

"Now unto him that is able to do exceeding abundantly above all that we ask or think, according to the power that worketh in us" (Ephesians 3:20). No matter the degree of your setback, God will do far beyond what you can ask or imagine (Ephesians 3:20). What you thought had no apparent use in your life, will be found to be the very thing used to change and heal others as you keep going forward in life. He will use it to build something great at His appointed time.

CHAPTER 11:

His Truth—The Perspective Helper

The major key to developing the right perspective on life's challenges is a constant view of God's Word. It is your constant view of your end and expectation. "This *is* my comfort in my affliction (depression, misery, or trouble): for thy word hath quickened me" (Psalms 119:50). It feels as if your trial is going to kill you, however, the truth is you will live and not die to declare the works of your Father. You don't see how it is going to come true, but you keep moving because you believe in something—you believe in what He says.

Your mind is not occupied with Satan's lies, but you abide in God's truth. You know what God says about you, and it is life to you. "It is the spirit that quickeneth; the flesh profiteth nothing: the words that I speak unto you, they are spirit, and they are life" (John 6:63). You don't become another man, full of fear, anger and frustration in the face of adversity. You don't become another woman in the face of turmoil and a lack of security. His perspective is yours. His Word will comfort you. It will fill your tank, build you and quicken you. It keeps you handling your affairs with character. It lights your path. It changes how you think. It will show you that He faithfully stands by you. His Word empowers you to act and go through whatever you are going through, not giving a temporary circumstance your permanent attention. "For ever, O LORD, thy word is settled in heaven" (Psalms 119:89).

CHAPTER 12:

Living it Daily

"The thief cometh not, but for to steal, and to kill, and to destroy: I am come that they might have life, and that they might have it more abundantly" (John 10:10). Life was given to be enjoyed. It is to be seen as time spent moving toward the plan of God. It is our greatest blessing and it is good, which is why He gives it in abundance. It is your day and you're glad in it (Psalm 118:24). You are determined to live the one life you've been given, and you will not be denied what He promised. You overcome evil with good. You are too positive to be negative. You are too humble to give room to pride. You forgive too quickly to be offended. You repent too quickly to be ashamed and condemned. You love unity too much to be divided. You have too much joy to lack strength. You have too much favor to be refused. You have too much God to be stopped. Live your days with no regrets, even with resolving all issues. Have a focused mind. Gladly love God, others and yourself, which we owe (Romans 13:8)

"All the days of the desponding *and* afflicted are made evil [by anxious thoughts and forebodings], but he who has a glad heart has a continual feast [regardless of circumstances]" (Proverbs 15:15, Amp). Daily live on the continual feast of God's goodness and mercy. Enjoy your daily progress and process. Celebrate your small victories and accomplishments. Rest and take vacations when needed. Smile and laugh! Hang out with others. Seek God to lead and guide you. Go deeper into the purpose or reason He created you—a purpose-filled day will make up a purpose-filled life. Share Jesus! Give, pour into and bless someone else.

Treat yourself to something good.   Live!
Everything that has been mentioned, every good
work, every good thing, is God's desire, which
sounds familiar to what we already desire, but
much more. He didn't come to take your life, but
to make it better. Allow nothing to detour you
from a promised, abundant life.

He is Very Present

There will be a pull every day to be absent in the
past or present right now and moving forward.
Dwelling on the past will eventually lead you into
living in it. We can either be absent in past and
its' physical burdens about the unchangeable, or
be present in His truth that nothing is too hard
for Him to recover. We can be absent looking for
a blessing, or be thankful to God that we're
blessed already. You will bulldoze the enemy out
of your way every time you decide to live forward,
refusing to be shackled today. At the moment of

every encounter, every mistake we make, every problem, every disagreement, our attitude is to forget what was done, press beyond the feelings and respond with a godly, forward action.

"Surely goodness and mercy shall follow me all the days of my life: and I will dwell in the house of the LORD for ever" (Psalms 23:6). David said "surely", knowing this to be true: Goodness and mercy would follow him every day. This implies that whatever happens, he knew God would be there. All God commands us to do is go forward, regardless of our emotions, circumstances and challenges. They both will be there to help us. Psalms 46:1 says, "God is our refuge and strength, a very present help in trouble." He is present right now to meet your true need. As a good father is present, so is our heavenly Father. He's not absent, but present to be all-wise and all-powerful. He was present before the trouble came to deliver you. He is present to help and guide you through it. He can and will empower you—today.

The Way Out

Trials and temptation may come as you press forward, yet with God, there is <u>always</u> a way. "There hath no temptation taken you but such as is common to man: but God is faithful, who will not suffer you to be tempted above that ye are able; but will with the temptation also make a way to escape, that ye may be able to bear it" (1 Corinthians 10:13). With God, just as the temptation exists, there is always a way of escape that exists and nothing is too overpowering to keep us from it. It is a matter of finding God's forward action. Only He saves. "I, even I, am the Lord; and besides Me there is no savior" (Isaiah 43:11). As we seek Him in prayer and His Word, He will show us His way of doing things. By His wisdom, He provides the way to life and favor (Proverbs 8:35).

Ultimately, the daily challenges we encounter are to prevent the bigger goal, which is fulfilling our purpose to advance God's kingdom and to walk in His promises. Be forward and resolve all issues, fully aware of the bigger picture. Whether it is financially or relationally, when dilemmas happen, pray for the specific wisdom for the way out, which He freely gives.

CHAPTER 13:

Ruling Over Your Thoughts

"For the weapons of our warfare are not carnal but mighty in God for pulling down (demolition of) strongholds, casting down arguments and every high thing that exalts itself against the knowledge of God, bringing every thought into captivity to the obedience of Christ, and being ready to punish all disobedience when your obedience is fulfilled" (2 Corinthians 10:4-6). Let's say someone comes to live with you to stay for a day, and you welcome them to make themselves at home. The moment you leave to pick up a few things from the grocery store, they begin to vandalize your house. They bust your windows, put holes in the walls, tare down your valuable wall paintings, and spill dark-colored juice on your expensive carpet. The bathroom sinks are damaged and food is all over the kitchen. You left for one brief moment and someone you allowed inside did the unthinkable, and now multiple, lengthy repairs are needed to correct all of the damages.

This is what evil imaginations and thoughts that rise up against the knowledge of God come to do. If you allow any contrary thoughts in, they will mess up your day, your mind, your emotions, your peace and your faith. In time, they will eventually derail and rob you of God's perfect will for your life. The knowledge of God is what He has said about you, your challenges, and your future. This is why God commands us to take **every** thought captive and He leaves no place for any other action.

Take authority over your mind. Catch yourself if you find any evil thoughts and any high thing trying to develop. Do not allow them to make themselves at home in your life. Philippians 4:8 tells us the type of thoughts to think on instead: "Finally, brethren, whatsoever things are true, whatsoever things *are* honest, whatsoever things *are* just, whatsoever things *are* pure, whatsoever things *are* lovely, whatsoever things *are* of good report; if *there be* any virtue, and if *there be* any praise, think on these things." Whatever you can find that is good, dwell on it and speak it. Think on what God has already done and what He is going to do, which is His Word. There is an abundance of promises from God there. If you work His Word, it will work for you. We have to move from dwelling on what has happened, into purposely thinking on the God Who will make something happen.

CHAPTER 14:

The Double

Beyond your God-directed action is the double
and it is your due reward for your obedience.
"For your shame *ye shall have* double; and *for*
confusion they shall rejoice in their portion:
therefore in their land they shall possess the
double: everlasting joy shall be unto them" (Isaiah
61:7). He has prepared for us double for any
shame and pain from our past. God truly does
have blessings awaiting you, yet only in the land
beyond your Red Sea. Only there will you
increase more and more, you and your children.
Only there will everything work. Everything
works there as God intended, including you. You
work! You don't have to pretend or long to be
like someone else, because in your land, you work.
We find ourselves walking in the person we have

so desired to one day break forth. Only there will revelation of God's Word and His power pour without restraint into your life.

It will not and cannot elude you. People to help and bless are there. In your land, wisdom and resources are there. Opportunities, relationships and honor are there. Only in that land will there be nothing missing and nothing broken. Abraham didn't receive God's promises until He obeyed God and left where he was, into the land that God had showed him. "Now the LORD had said unto Abram, Get thee out of thy country, and from thy kindred, and from thy father's house, unto a land that I will shew thee: And I will make of thee a great nation, and I will bless thee, and make thy name great; and thou shalt be a blessing: And I will bless them that bless thee, and curse him that curseth thee: and in thee shall all families of the earth be blessed" (Genesis 12:1-3).

CHAPTER 15:

Time to Finish, Time to Live

"When Jesus therefore had received the vinegar, he said, It is finished: and he bowed his head, and gave up the ghost" (John 19:30). In light of all we know we have done, we can find it difficult to comprehend what He simply says, "It is finished". Jesus finished, so we can finish. Jesus is our greatest example of moving forward. He moved forward and died. Dare we not move forward and live? Since He overcame, we now overcome through Him and live a forward life. If He lives in you, He will help you forward to finish. Do not look for the encouragement regarding whether you can do it. Do not look for the pat on your shoulder. Do not yearn for the approval of men. It is not a requirement or prerequisite to the forward life. This is your race. Run with confidence, joy and authority. It's your prize and

God is all you need to obtain it. Your blessing comes in moving forward. He is waiting to bless the work of our hands. He is waiting to give you all that He promised. Move forward.

Moving forward *is* your deliverance. Moving forward *is* your breakthrough.

Salvation

God desires for you to not perish, but to repent and receive the free gift of salvation through Jesus Christ. He will be all that you need and more.

Romans 5:11-12 "And not only so, but we also joy in God through our Lord Jesus Christ, by whom we have now received the atonement (exchange). Wherefore, as by one man sin entered into the world, and death by sin; and so death passed upon all men, for that all have sinned."

Romans 6:23 "For the wages of sin is death; but the gift of God is eternal life through Jesus Christ our Lord."

Romans 10:9-10 "That if thou shalt confess with thy mouth the Lord Jesus, and shalt believe in thine heart that God hath raised him from the dead, thou shalt be saved. For with the heart man believeth unto righteousness; and with the mouth confession is made unto salvation."

Prayer this pray with me:

Dear God, I realize I am in need of a savior and You gave Your Son as atonement or exchange for me. Forgive me of all my sin. I confess with my mouth the Lord Jesus and that He lives. Come Savior and live in me. Come Lord and lead me. I am now saved. In Jesus' Name, Amen.

Welcome to Newness of Life

Now that you have made a decision to receive Jesus into your heart, God can now show you His ways, provide you His truth and give you abundant life. He will help you forget the old and receive the new.

2 Corinthians 5:17 "Therefore if any man be in Christ, he is a new creature: old things are passed away; behold, all things are become new. '

John 10:9-11 "I am the door: by me if any man enter in, he shall be saved, and shall go in and out, and find pasture. The thief cometh not, but for to steal, and to kill, and to destroy: I am come that they might have life, and that they might have it more abundantly.

Change Your Mind

To become a millionaire, you must think like a millionaire. To become like Christ, you must think like Christ. Begin to learn of Him and rest in His ways. Change your mind with God's Word, and you will see the transformation and joy in your life you want.

Matthew 11:29 "Take my yoke upon you, and learn of me; for I am meek and lowly in heart: and ye shall find rest unto your souls."

Romans 12:2 "And be not conformed to this world: but be ye transformed by the renewing of your mind, that ye may prove what is that good, and acceptable, and perfect, will of God."

Isaiah 26:3 "Thou wilt keep him in perfect peace, whose mind is stayed on thee: because he trusteth in thee."

Psalm 84:5, 12 "Blessed is the man whose strength is in thee; in whose heart are the ways of them. O LORD of hosts, blessed (happy!) is the man that trusteth in thee."

Psalm 1:2-3 "But his delight is in the law of the LORD; and in his law doth he meditate day and night. And he shall be like a tree planted by the rivers of water, that bringeth forth his fruit in his season; his leaf also shall not wither; and whatsoever he doeth shall prosper."

Just Do It

True change will require something of you. It is your responsibility to spend time with God and His Word. It's your responsibility to act on what He says. Do it and you will see God, by His Spirit and grace, do great things with you and for you.

James 1:22-25 "But be ye doers of the word, and not hearers only, deceiving your own selves. For if any be a hearer of the word, and not a doer, he is like unto a man beholding his natural face in a glass: For he beholdeth himself, and goeth his way, and straightway forgetteth what manner of man he was. But whoso looketh into the perfect law of liberty, and continueth therein, he being not a forgetful hearer, but a doer of the work, this man shall be blessed in his deed."

John 13:17 "If ye know these things, happy are ye if ye do them."

Proverbs 13:4 "The soul of the sluggard desireth, and hath nothing: but the soul of the diligent shall be made fat."

Romans 1:17 "For therein is the righteousness of God revealed from faith to faith: as it is written, The just shall live by faith."

About the Author

Bernard Trippett is a husband and father of four beautiful children. His love for writing began his freshman year at Georgia Southern University when he was assigned to take a remedial English course and was elevated to Honors. He later graduated and continued to develop his God-given gift for writing, becoming a professional business writer and a published author.

He went on to graduate from Word of Faith Bible Training Center and is a licensed minister of the Gospel of the Lord Jesus Christ. His passion is in demonstrating and teaching others how to walk in the power of God, become fully acquainted with His love, and how to reverence the Lord and understand His character. He enjoys ministering to the heart and encouraging others toward a rewarding life of obedience.

He has served in ministerial roles, such as: men's ministry, campus ministry president, assistant youth pastor, armor bearer, prayer counselor and is currently a staff minister at the Body of Christ Assemblies Church in Statesboro, GA.

Purpose

The purpose of the *Power Books Series* is to quicken and empower you spiritually to act on God's Word. They are like spiritual energy drinks, designed to pull you out and pull you forward. If you do not want to be convicted, chastised and inspired to change, do not pick up a power book. They will cause what you need to hear, to become what you want to hear. Jesus said I am the way, the truth and the life. Power Books will reveal His ways. Power Books will tell you the truth. Power Books will equip you to obtain the abundant life God prepared for you before you came. You can do it! You just need some power.

For more information, please visit www.powerbookministries.com.

Made in the USA
Las Vegas, NV
14 May 2021